D0017854

what EVERYONE SHOULD KNOW ABOUT MONEY

before they enter THE REAL WORLD

JOSEPH SANGL

NIN Publishing

Cover design by Chris Dunagan

Library of Congress Control Number: 2009938229

Sangl, Joseph

ISBN 978-1-61623-797-4

First Edition

Printed in the United States by Morris Publishing®
3212 East Highway 30
Kearney, NE 68847
1-800-650-7888

To my daughter, Melea, who inspired me to write this book.

TABLE OF CONTENTS

PREFACE

I used to be broke. My bank account balance usually hovered around $4.13, and I celebrated because it was positive! My financial story began the first day of my high school senior year. I knew that I was going to attend college because the idea of obtaining a full-time job immediately after high school graduation was very unappealing.

For the past year, I had received about 17,000 brochures from various colleges and universities. Each one attempted to convince me to attend their school. I knew my college decision would make a huge impact on the rest of my life, but I had no idea how to decide which school I should attend.

As I walked into the halls of Southwestern High School the first day of my senior year, I saw an application for Purdue University sitting just outside the guidance counselor's office. There was no application fee, so I picked up a copy.

I had no idea what subject I should study, but in my calculus class I heard the teacher say that there was going to be strong demand for engineers in the next five years. He followed that by saying that engineers are paid an excellent salary.

I grew up in Indiana, so I was very aware that Purdue had an outstanding engineering school. I pulled out the application and filled it out. In the section stating "school you are applying to", I checked "School of Engineering." I noticed a statement on the application that it would be several months before I would receive their decision.

It was only about seven days later that I received a letter from Purdue University with "Congratulations!" printed on the outside. The letter informed me that I was accepted to the school of engineering. Since Purdue was a great school, and they had already accepted me, I did not apply to another school.

I graduated from high school in the spring and began getting ready to attend college. It was a very exciting time as I prepared to move away from home for the first time in my life. I was ready to take on the world. I had a few scholarships, but they did not come close to paying for tuition, room and board, books and fees. As I looked for ways to pay for the rest of my college bills, I was encouraged to apply for financial assistance using the FAFSA (Free Application for Federal Student Aid). It was an easy application process, and shortly afterward a ton of student loans were approved for me. This decision would have a major impact on my life.

I arrived on campus about a week before fall classes began to start working a part-time job in the residence hall cafeteria. With 37,000 students on a single campus, I met a lot of new friends. I met people from all over the world. It was awesome! I also met my future bride that first weekend of college.

I was also met by something I was not prepared for – credit card companies. They had people scattered throughout the campus, and each one was offering free Purdue gear in exchange for filling out their credit card application. I did not fill out ONE of them; I filled out ALL of them.

I received free t-shirts, two-liters of soda, frisbees and various other trinkets. I never dreamed I would be approved to receive a credit card. After all, I had NO money and almost zero income!

In spite of that, it was just a short while before my first credit card showed up. It was a fancy-looking black plastic card that had a metal fleck finish. It said "ADVANTA" across the top. They said they were excited to offer me this credit card, and all I had to do was call the number on the front to activate it. I did so immediately and put the card into my pocket. This decision would have a major impact on my life.

I graduated just four short years later with a degree in mechanical engineering, a mountain of student loan debt and credit card debt.

To reward myself for graduating college, I wanted to upgrade my vehicle. I purchased a used truck with no down payment – 100 percent financing.

I proposed to my college sweetheart, Jenn, and she said, "Yes!" I financed the engagement and wedding rings.

Jenn graduated from Purdue a year after I did, and I wanted to give her an amazing graduation gift. I bought her a brand new car. I had no money, so I financed the entire purchase price – including the sales tax. It was amazing to give her the new car, but the payments for the next 48 months were not so amazing.

We were married in June 1997. One year later, I accepted a job transfer to South Carolina. We had very little money, but we managed to buy a house. This was debt of an incredibly different type – it had six figures!

Do you see the trend? We were making great decisions with our lives by attending and finishing college, marrying each other, and obtaining good jobs, but we were making poor money decisions.

We spent our twenties earning excellent money, but piling up debt even faster. When we were 28 years old, we had what I call an "IHHE Moment." An IHHE Moment is an "I Have Had Enough!" Moment. We knew we had to change the way that we were managing our money, or we were going to live a life full of regrets.

We made massive changes to the way we managed our finances and became debt-free except for our house. We have lived free of debt ever since! It is incredible how much of an impact money, or the lack of it, can have on relationships and fulfilling one's calling.

As we walked out of our financial mistakes, Jenn and I learned a lot about how we can ensure that we make wise decisions with money. It is my hope that this book will help you prosper and avoid making some of the poor decisions we made. Although the principles taught in this book are relevant to every person who deals with money, my primary audience for this book are those who are preparing to enter the "real world" for the first time. A place where things like house payments, utilities and car repairs exist.

It is an exciting and scary time, and you have a great chance of prospering in life if you apply the principles taught in this book. It is what I think everyone should know about money before they enter the real world.

I hope this book *helps you accomplish far more than you ever thought possible with your personal finances.*

Chapter ONE

Plan For Life

Everyone Should Know ...
Written plans, hopes and dreams are more likely to come true than those that are unwritten.

What do you want to accomplish during your lifetime? What have you been put on earth to do?

As you embark into life in the real world, there is no doubt that you have been asking yourself these questions. Sometimes these questions can cause one to feel overwhelmed or fearful. Other times, these questions can fill one with hope and joy. You may be experiencing all of these feelings.

Every person has hopes and dreams they want to achieve. I believe every person has been put on Earth for a specific purpose, and I want you to be able to accomplish your hopes and dreams. Most people, however, do not have a written plan for how they are going to achieve their dreams. In fact, more than 50 percent of people who attend one of our personal finance teaching experiences have never written their hopes and dreams on paper. This is very sad.

Henry Ford once said, "Fail to plan. Plan to fail." This is an incredibly true statement.

I clearly remember the day I was teaching the Financial Learning Experience in a small town. I asked everyone in the room to write their hopes and dreams on paper. When they had finished this task, I asked them this question – "If this is the first time you have ever written down your hopes and dreams in your adult life, please raise your hand."

As usual, more than half of the room raised a hand, but one person's hand caught my attention more than the others. It was a man who was over 70 years old and still working a full-time factory job to produce an income for his family. He was working **because he had to**. I wonder if he would still be working full-time at 70 if he would have written down his hopes and dreams on paper when he was 18.

You have huge potential. What do you want to make sure you accomplish during your lifetime? Please take the next few minutes to write down your hopes, plans and dreams on the form on the next page. As you think through them, use the list of ideas on the next page to stimulate your thoughts.

I BEG you to write down some of your hopes and dreams before reading the rest of this book. Be sure to write down your crazy dreams too. The dreams that others might laugh and sneer at CAN come true!

Hopes and Dreams Ideas

Travel	College degree	Great marriage
Awesome children	Own a house	Run a marathon
Win with money	Own a car	Have a good job
Life-changing work	Start a business	Make great friends
Give a lot of money away	Help the poor	Write a song
Play professional sports	Be physically fit for life	Learn a foreign language
Learn to play an instrument	Write a book	Hike a tall mountain
Become a missionary	Run with Pamplona bulls	Start a church
Whitewater rafting	Parachute out of an airplane	Get my pilot's license
Visit Elvis' grave	Watch July 4th fireworks at Mount Rushmore	Retire by age 50
Start a charity	Direct a movie	See Egyptian pyramids
Visit Rome	Go to Paris	Visit the Taj Mahal
Go to London	Australia	New Zealand
Grand Canyon	Yellowstone	Redwoods of California
Attend Indy 500	Attend Daytona 500	Fashion Show in NYC
Write a movie script	Stand on the rim of an active volcano	Live in downtown Chicago for two years
Start a plant nursery	Catch a shark	Stand on all seven continents
Walk on the moon	Walk on Mars	Get married
Dig a well in Africa	Give away $1 million	Have children
Work for free	Shop in Paris	Adopt a child

My Hopes and Dreams

Hopes and Dreams	Cost

What was it like to write your dreams? What feelings did you experience? Was this the first time you have written down your thoughts like this?

I have found it is absolutely essential to write mine down, or I will lose track and completely forget about them. It would be terrible to forget about them – they are *my* hopes and dreams. I am much more likely to accomplish my written goals during my lifetime.

I hope you included some totally outrageous dreams in your list. It is fun to dream, and someday the crazy dream might just come true. I, personally, have a dream to start a university. It might sound crazy, but it has a chance of happening because I have a plan. Hope keeps me motivated.

I also have a dream to be an NBA basketball player. This dream seems to have passed me by, but I am OK with that. Maybe I will change the dream to owning an NBA team!

It is important to continue updating and revising this list throughout your life. Events in life will sometime change your focus as you are exposed to things that you never knew existed. It is important to add those new ideas to your list.

Everyone Should Know ...
Planned money accomplishes more than unplanned money.

Have you ever started out the day with a twenty dollar bill in your pocket and arrived home at the end of the day with a crumpled one dollar bill and a few coins? If someone asked you where all of the money went, it would be difficult to remember where most of it went, right?

This has occurred countless times in my life because I am a spender. This means that if any money makes it into my pocket without a plan, it has little chance for survival. I have found that my money accomplishes much more when I prepare a plan before I actually spend it.

It is very important to maximize the use of each dollar because most plans, hopes and dreams cost money. Some dreams may cost very little; Many will cost a substantial amount.

Before you continue reading, I challenge you to go back to your hopes and dreams list and put an estimated cost next to each one. It does not have to be an exact number, just an educated guess. It might be frightening to see the amount of money required to achieve your list, but hopefully, it should also help you clearly understand the importance of having a plan for your money.

As a former broke person who managed to spend all of his money every month without saving for anything, I can tell you that my family's written goals are THE REASON that we have been able to accomplish more of our plans, hopes and dreams than I ever thought possible.

As a high school student, I worked for my father building homes, and he paid me a great hourly wage. There were times when I was focused on purchasing a specific item, and there were times when I was totally unfocused. Guess what? The money disappeared when I was unfocused. When I was focused, I had nice purchases to show for the money I had earned.

I remember a specific house we built. We were laying brick in the smoking hot summer sun. My job was to carry bricks, mix mortar and joint out the brick once it was laid. It was brutal weather, so we would start at sunrise so we could finish by the time it was becoming unbearably hot.

This does not sound like fun work, but it was fun because I was highly focused on a new item that I wanted to purchase – the item was a new camera. A Pentax K-1000 to be exact. It was a rocking 35 mm camera with a removable lens. I can not remember its exact cost, but it was somewhere around two hundred dollars.

I willing to work a tough job in super hot weather because I knew my labor was not in vain. I knew there was a nice purchase ahead of me. Hard work and planning led to a rewarding purchase.

Another great purchase was a motorcycle. My twin brother and I really wanted a motorcycle. We lived out in the country, and a motorcycle would be a great way to explore our farm and beyond. Our father came up with a great way for us to earn the money to purchase it.

In one of the farm fields, we grew soybeans. The field was producing a fabulous crop of weeds that year. Dad said he would pay us one penny for every weed we pulled or cut down. We pulled enough weeds to buy the motorcycle. It was a Honda C-70 Passport, and it was awesome! Good planning and hard work once again led to a rewarding purchase.

You might have noticed that I have not shared a single story where I did not plan my spending. This is because I have no idea where the money went – it was unplanned and it disappeared without a trace!

Chapter TWO

Plan The Money

Everyone Should Know ...
Income – Outgo = Exactly Zero

I believe that it is EZ to win with money. You might not believe me, but I can prove it. It is as simple as recognizing this basic fact:

INCOME – OUTGO = EXACTLY ZERO

If the first letter of each word is used to show this formula, we obtain the following:

I – O = EZ

I told you it was EZ – **E**xactly **Z**ero! If your OUTGO exceeds your INCOME, the result is no longer EXACTLY ZERO. It now yields a negative result.

You will not prosper with money if you continually spend more than you make. One can certainly live this way for a while by addressing the negative number with debt. The debt option will eventually run out, and all of it must be paid back.

Jenn and I were B-R-O-K-E. We had college degrees and jobs, but we were broke because we failed to recognize the truth of INCOME – OUTGO = EXACTLY ZERO.

We did not recognize how EZ it was to win with our money until December 2002. We had our IHHE Moment and from that day forward, we started winning with our finances. We did it by spending our money on paper before it was spent for real.

It really is EZ!

Everyone Should Know ...
Spend your money on paper BEFORE it is spent for real.

I do not know how much money you earn or are given, but we have already covered the fact that planned money accomplishes more than unplanned money.

You might receive $10 a month. You might receive $5,000 a month. Regardless of the amount, it is important to plan where the money should go before it is spent for real.

If I said I would give you $200 with the single stipulation that you must first plan where it would be spent, would you do it? I know I would take that deal.

How long does it really take to plan your spending? Five minutes? Thirty minutes? It certainly does not take very long. If you plan your spending on paper BEFORE you spend it for real, you will make much wiser decisions and maximize the use of your money.

Impulsively spending money without a plan leads to empty pockets and little to show for it. Planning before actually spending the money leads to a healthy savings account, giving and rewarding purchases.

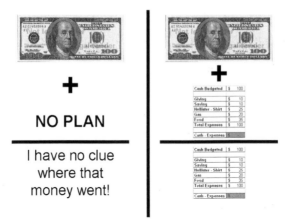

Spend your money on paper before it is spent for real.

Plan your spending before you actually spend the money. I can not emphasize this one point enough. If you learn nothing else from this book, I hope this is what you take with you and apply for the rest of your life. It takes just a few minutes to plan your spending and ensure that your money is best utilized.

Ensure that INCOME – OUTGO = EXACTLY ZERO every single time you receive money. Be sure to include giving, saving and some fun spending every time.

Do you have some money right now? Use the next five minutes to prepare a plan for how that money will be utilized. You can visit IWasBrokeNowImNot.com and click on "Free Tools" to find a great Mini-Budget tool. A pencil, paper and a calculator also works well.

Consider an example using the Mini-Budget. Suppose I have received $200 for working at Taco Bell this month (I loved working at Taco Bell). I can visit IWasBrokeNowImNot.com, and click on "Free Tools" and "Mini-Budget" to get the free budgeting tool.

The following Mini-Budget appears.

Cash Budgeted	
Expense 1	
Expense 2	
Expense 3	
Expense 4	
Expense 5	
Expense 6	
Total Expenses	
INCOME – OUTGO =	$ -

I enter $200 into the row that states "Cash Budgeted" and INCOME – OUTGO no longer equals EXACTLY ZERO. This means there is unplanned money. We must spend our money on paper before we spend it for real because unplanned money means there is a greater chance of impulsively spending.

Cash Budgeted	$	200
Expense 1		
Expense 2		
Expense 3		
Expense 4		
Expense 5		
Expense 6		
Total Expenses	$	-
INCOME – OUTGO =	$	200

Giving is a huge part of my life, and it is important to me to give away at least 10 percent of my money. I enter $20 into the plan. We now have $180 of unplanned money remaining.

Cash Budgeted	$	200
Give 10% away	$	20
Expense 2		
Expense 3		
Expense 4		
Expense 5		
Expense 6		
Total Expenses	$	20
INCOME – OUTGO =	$	180

I also want to support a charity that helps poor children receive medical care so I designate $10 for that charity.

Cash Budgeted	$	200
Give 10% away	$	20
Children's Medical Charity	$	10
Expense 3		
Expense 4		
Expense 5		
Expense 6		
Total Expenses	$	30
INCOME – OUTGO =	$	170

Generosity matters! I have found the greatest thing I can do with money is give it away to causes I really believe in.

What are some causes you really believe in that you could financially support? Every dollar matters. Even if you can only give a few dollars, do not minimize the importance of your gift. It makes a huge difference! I am also saving for college books and a summer vacation I want to take with my friends. I "spend" $50 for each item.

Cash Budgeted	$	200
Give 10% away	$	20
Children's Medical Charity	$	10
Books For College (Savings)	$	50
Summer Trip (Savings)	$	50
Expense 5		
Expense 6		
Total Expenses	$	130
INCOME – OUTGO =	$	70

I "spent" some money into savings. Have you ever thought of saving money as spending? It truly is spending your money. When you spend money into savings, you forfeit the right to spend the money at the mall. This was something I did not fully comprehend until my late twenties. When I finally grasped this concept, I began to pile up some money in my savings account!

Continuing with the example, I include the $40 cost of a new pair of jeans that I really want.

Cash Budgeted	$	200
Give 10% away	$	20
Children's Medical Charity	$	10
Books For College (Savings)	$	50
Summer Trip (Savings)	$	50
Jeans	$	40
Expense 6		
Total Expenses	$	170
INCOME – OUTGO =	$	30

I also want to have some fun, so I put $60 into the plan for food, movies and gas.

Cash Budgeted	$	200
Give 10% away	$	20
Children's Medical Charity	$	10
Books For College (Savings)	$	50
Summer Trip (Savings)	$	50
Jeans	$	40
Food/Movies/Gas	$	60
Total Expenses	$	230
INCOME – OUTGO =	$	(30)

The spending plan is now showing a negative $30. I wanted $60 for food, movies and gas, but that caused our spending plan to become negative. I can not do that and win with my money. I must make a decision on the items that will be funded and the ones which won't.

Welcome to life. A place where we would all love to spend without thinking about it, but reality requires that we make choices. We can not fund everything we want this month, so we must make decisions. Some decisions will be difficult, but they will be way less difficult than being broke!

In this example, I decided to adjust my spending to $30 on jeans and $40 dollars on food, movies and gas. This enables the Mini-Budget to become EZ – EXACTLY ZERO.

Cash Budgeted	$	200
Give 10% away	$	20
Children's Medical Charity	$	10
Books For College (Savings)	$	50
Summer Trip (Savings)	$	50
Jeans	$	30
Food/Movies/Gas	$	40
Total Expenses	$	200
INCOME – OUTGO =	$	-

Will an EZ spending plan allow you to purchase everything you could possibly want in life? The answer is a resounding, "NO!", but it will help ensure that you fund the things most important to you.

I have found that I am afflicted with a problem of wanting more than I can afford. For every dollar I have, I want to spend it in five different places. Do you have that problem? I will not spend more than I have, so I must make choices.

You must make decisions. Sometimes they will be easy. Other times will be more difficult, but I can promise you that when you spend your money on paper before you really spend the money, more of your hopes and dreams will be funded.

My family prepares a written spending plan every month before the money arrives and before the month begins. If you make it a consistent habit to spend your money on paper before you spend it for real and apply INCOME – OUTGO = EXACTLY ZERO, you will maximize your financial resources.

Everyone Should Know ...
Income is important!

This is really the biggest no-brainer in the history of personal finance, but I am regularly surprised by people who refuse to recognize this fundamental fact.

In order for INCOME – OUTGO = EXACTLY ZERO, there must be income! I have had people get mad at me because I have told them that they need to get a job. They make statements like, "I will not be paid what I am worth." Some people become frustrated with the lack of high-paying employment options available to them so they choose to produce zero income instead. The result is a financial mess that worsens every day.

Income provides the opportunity for outgo. It is just that simple. My hero, Dave Ramsey, says it this way, "There is a good place to go when you are broke – to WORK! It is a sure-fired money making scheme."

If you are frustrated with your lack of ability to produce income, seek out job skills and training that the business world needs. I am just guessing here, but I believe that a degree in four-eyed frog hair dissection will not be in high demand in the future. However, with an aging population in the United States, the healthcare profession will be booming.

Without income, there will be no outgo without eroding a savings account or increasing debt. Income is a must.

Chapter **THREE**

Always Give

Everyone Should Know ...
Giving is AWESOME!

There is clear evidence that piles of money do not ensure happiness. We have all met people who have plenty of money, but are far from happy. Achieving wealth can certainly be a goal, but one is in for a really sad surprise if he or she believes that it will solve all of life's complex issues.

Why do you want to win with your money? I am betting that it is not so you can swim in money like Scrooge McDuck. Even more, I believe you want to win with your money so you can accomplish your hopes, plans and dreams (I hope you wrote some down earlier).

I challenge you to ensure that your goals include giving to worthwhile causes that you believe in. Giving is the greatest reward one can receive for being a wise with his/her money.

There is *nothing* like helping someone else achieve a dream that they had little or no chance of accomplishing on their own. There is *nothing* like funding a cause that you desperately and fiercely believe in. There is *nothing* like helping the poor. There is *nothing* like blessing someone with a financial gift simply because you believe in them.

Jenn and I know what it is like to give. We have been able to give to causes we are passionate about because we have been blessed and have chosen to manage our money well.

We also know the blessing of receiving. We have received amazing gifts that have powerfully impacted our lives.

It is very easy to fall into the trap of placing all of one's happiness and security in money. Jake Beaty, a pastor at NewSpring Church in Anderson, S.C., once asked our mutual friend, Jamie Salmon, this question – "Jamie, why do you give?"

Jamie's response rocked my world so much that I want to share it in this book. His response? "I give to keep from being selfish." Well said, Jamie. Well said.

To whom should you give money? Think back over your life. Who or what has made an impact on your life? Perhaps there is a cause you are passionate about and would love to support.

Your church is a great place to give. Maybe you are passionate about helping children with juvenile diabetes and want to support research for a cure. The United Way provides amazing help throughout the nation, as does the American Red Cross. Local food banks and homeless shelters always need financial and volunteer support. Local youth programs also operate on other's generous donations. Find somewhere to give and make it a high priority to consistently provide financial help.

Here are questions I consider when determining who I will support financially.

- Has this organization made a difference in my life?
- Is this organization making a difference in people's lives?
- Is this organization managing their resources well? Even more importantly, is this organization above reproach in all of its dealings?
- Will my gift make a difference?

Everyone Should Know ...
How to begin giving.

You can ensure that you give on a consistent basis by preparing a written spending plan every time you receive money. The act of preparing a written spending plan provides a regular and consistent opportunity for you to give money away.

If you receive a regular paycheck, it is possible for you to contribute money directly from each paycheck. You can also set up a monthly bank account draft.

I challenge you to start giving now, and make it a habit for the rest of your life. Even if you can only give five dollars a month, do it now. If you wait until you have enough money to give, it is highly unlikely that you will ever begin.

Giving is the most rewarding part of my life.

Chapter FOUR

Always Save

Everyone Should Know ...
Saving prevents financial disasters.

I love the story about Joseph and Pharaoh in ancient Egypt. Pharaoh had a crazy dream he could not understand, and Joseph was called to help him interpret its meaning. Joseph said that there would be seven years of plenty, which would be immediately followed by seven years of famine.

Pharaoh immediately put Joseph in charge of preparing for the seven years of famine. Joseph issued a requirement that 20 percent of each year's harvest was to be saved during the seven plentiful years.

A 20 percent annual savings rate. One fifth of everything. Considering the United States savings rate has hovered at nearly 0 percent for the past decade, 20 percent is an outrageously high amount.

The seven years of abundance and seven years of famine happened just as Joseph had interpreted. The Egyptians saved just as they had been instructed and disaster was averted. The super high savings rate protected Egypt during a horrible economic time.

I love this story because it shows the power of saving! The moral is clear – when times are good, be sure to prepare for tougher times. The tougher times WILL come. When times are good, it is so easy to become accustomed to living it up and forget that tough times will come.

Saving helps prevent financial emergencies. When I had no money in savings, I was always experiencing a financial emergency. My car would break down, and I would have a financial emergency. My refrigerator would break down, and I would have a financial emergency. My friends would make last-minute plans to drive to the Purdue football game against Wisconsin in downtown Madison, and I would have a financial emergency.

When Jenn and I made savings a top priority, we stopped having financial emergencies. When the car breaks down; we fix it. When we fall ill; we have money to pay the doctor.

A lack of saved money leads to financial emergencies. More importantly, it can lead to stress, broken relationships and broken promises. Make it a practice to save every single time you receive money. You will avoid a lot of heartache.

It is important to save for three important categories of expenses.

1. Emergencies
2. Known, Upcoming Expenses
3. Plans, Hopes and Dreams

Everyone Should Know ...
Save money for emergencies.

You will have emergencies; life is full of them. Most of them will cost money. You might have to travel home quickly for a family emergency. A once-in-a-lifetime opportunity might present itself to you, and it will cost money.

You might be required to purchase a textbook that was not listed. The car might break down. You could become sick and have to pay a doctor bill. You could lose your student loans or college funding. You might have to quit your job to accommodate a class.

It is clear that everyone will experience emergencies that cost money. Save for them so the stress of incurring new debt does not add to an already tough situation.

Everyone Should Know ...
Save money for known, upcoming expenses.

The car will break down. I do not know which part will break, but something will fail. It is a known, upcoming expense. Christmas will show up on December 25. Just as it has the past 2,000 years. Presents will need to be purchased. They are a known, upcoming expense.

Here are some additional known, upcoming expenses you might deal with now or in the future:
- Vacation
- Books for the upcoming semester
- Car tires
- Quarterly or annual insurance premiums
- Car property taxes
- New car
- One semester study-abroad program

I have learned the hard way that I need to save for these known, upcoming expenses. When I was broke, I failed to save for Christmas and ended up financing the presents with my credit card. Every. Single. Year.

It was a very tough cycle to break, but I was able to avoid the issue entirely by planning for these expenses and saving for them before they actually happened. Jenn and I save money every month for our known, upcoming expenses. It causes our monthly spending plan to have less available spending money, but it is worth the hassle because it allows us to focus on the JOY of giving Christmas presents instead of the AGONY of figuring out how to pay for them.

Everyone Should Know ...
Save money for dreams.

This is my favorite category of savings. It is nice to have money available to cover a financial emergency. It is awesome to have money available to pay cash for known, upcoming expenses like Christmas, car repairs and property taxes.

I am most passionate, however, about funding my family's dreams. This is why we invest the time necessary to plan our spending in such detail.

My family wants to travel to Australia and New Zealand. We want to give away a certain amount of money. We want our children to graduate from college without any student loan debt. We want to pay for their first house so they do not ever have any house debt.

It will take a lot of money to make these dreams come true. This is why we are so highly focused on maximizing every single dollar we are entrusted to manage.

Will we achieve all our dreams? I do not know, but we are certainly not going to be found guilty of laziness and sloppy money management. We are going to do everything we possibly can to fund them.

Make sure you are intentional about funding your plans, hopes and dreams. When you see them being funded, it will help you stick to your financial plan – even when times are tough.

Chapter FIVE

Avoid Debt

Everyone Should Know ...
Debt is the single largest cause of stress and financial problems.

Of all the problems I see people dealing with, debt is the single largest cause of stress and financial problems. Of course, nearly everyone who signs up for debt has the intention to repay it, but I have found that most people do not take the time to prepare a written spending plan. As a result, they do not recognize the reality of their financial situation when they agree to acquire additional debt.

I have seen people who are able to pay all of their bills on time, but when they sign up for another car payment or furniture payment everything falls apart. The strain of the payment took them by surprise because they failed to plan their finances.

Debt in and of itself is not wrong, but the fact that I have struggled with a pile of debt and the fact that I have counseled thousands of others on this topic tells me that debt should be very carefully considered before ever agreeing to sign the line.

Everyone Should Know ...
Debt can prevent me from achieving my dreams.

I have found that debt can prevent me from achieving my dreams. I have never had a person say, "Joe, I obtained a credit card, ran up a huge balance on it, and all of my dreams came true."

Instead, I hear sorrow and regret because their debt has run out of control and is now preventing many of their plans, hopes and dreams from being funded.

Have you ever owed money to anyone? I have owed credit cards. I have owed car finance companies. I have owed furniture and jewelry companies. I have owed student loan companies. I have owed mortgage companies. It was all terrible.

I have been able to eliminate all of the debt except for the home mortgage, and I am closing in on that one. I can tell you that there is substantially less stress on this side of my debt struggles.

Everyone Should Know ...
Debt is spending tomorrow's money today.

What is debt anyway? It is defined by Dictionary.com as "something that is owed or that one is bound to pay to or perform for another." I like to define debt another way.

Sangl's Definition Of Debt
Debt is spending tomorrow's money today.

Think about that definition for a moment.

What are some common items people use debt to purchase? Cars. Houses. Boats. Motorcycles. College education. Diamond rings. Pets. Furniture. Computers. Appliances. Cell phones. TVs. Vacations. Home repairs. Car repairs. Musical instruments. Many people pledge away their future income to obtain these items immediately.

One of the first debts many people obtain is car debt. Why would someone sign up for car debt? Because they do not have the money to pay for it when they purchase it. Is it a surprise that someone would need to purchase a car? For many young adults, it is a purchase they have been dreaming of since they were very young. It is not a surprise purchase, yet so few people save money for it. As a result, they choose to use debt to obtain it.

A loan is requested and the instant the loan papers are signed, that person has just spent some of tomorrow's money, next month's money, some of next year's money, and quite possibly, a portion of several year's worth of income.

Everyone Should Know ...
Debt is an enabler for impulsive spending decisions.

Visit a college campus on opening weekend of a fall semester, and you will see credit card applications galore. The credit card companies will give away free t-shirts, soda, frisbees and blankets to entice you to fill out an application. I filled out all of them, and I never dreamed that I would be approved because I had very little income. After all, I was a full-time college student. Despite these facts, a credit card showed up, and my impulsive spending decisions were enabled because I had a debt card (a.k.a. – credit card).

Debt is commonplace in America. It is readily available, and offered by nearly everyone who sells. Have you ever considered why so many businesses offer financing? It is because without financing, they would sell very little product because most people have little or no savings!

Why do car dealers offer financing? Because people are broke. Broke people will impulsively spend $20,000 in *loaned* money. Car dealers would sell very few cars if they did not offer financing and enable impulsive purchases.

I have observed that people who have saved $20,000 over a long period of time are highly unlikely to impulsively spend that money. On the contrary, they will demand to receive a huge bargain for them to spend the money. It is a fact that car dealers usually make less money on a cash purchase and more money on financed purchases.

Everyone Should Know ...
Debt can cause a loss of perspective.

People will agree to debt because they do not truly realize just how much they have agreed to repay. They are blinded by their goal, and this leads to a loss of perspective of the debt required to achieve it.

A classic example are student loans. Why do colleges offer student loans? Because people are broke, and very few people save money to pay for their children's college education.

Is it a surprise that many children go to college? NO! When my daughter was born, I was given an 18-year warning that she was going to college. As a result, I have been saving for my daughter's education.

Many parents have not heeded the warning, however, and have failed to save for their children's college education. This means many young people will make a decision to acquire debt so they can obtain their degree.

Many students will believe that debt is a forgone conclusion so they are not intimidated by the thought of debt. I have seen student loans of more than $80,000 obtained by a student who received a history degree. I have seen student loans of more than $50,000 for a student who received a degree in psychology.

The debt causes no immediate pain because repayment is not required until the student graduates. When repayment begins, the student realizes just how much they have financed. Many times the pain is made even greater by the fact that they could have obtained the exact same degree for a fourth of the cost by attending a technical or community college for the first two years.

Everyone Should Know ...
Debt robs people of their ability to give and save.

When one obtains debt and pledges away large chunks of their future income, it robs them of their ability to give and save. When $500 to $700 a month are being sent to the lenders, it can place a tremendous strain on one's ability to pay bills on time.

I have found this to be true in my own life. The lender knows it too. They know that if you have no savings, you will almost certainly remain in debt and continue to turn to lenders to finance future purchases.

I know a man who owned a car dealership. He said that he never allowed someone to pay off a car without calling them and inviting them down to the car lot. He would call them approximately six months before the car was paid off. His reason for calling? He said if people ever tasted freedom from car payments, it would be very difficult to sell them another car with car payments!

Everyone Should Know ...
Debt traps people in jobs they despise.

I regularly ask people what they have been put on earth to do. The most common response is, "I have no idea, but I KNOW it is definitely NOT what I am doing right now!"

They dislike their job, but are addicted to the income and trapped by their debt. As a result, they despise their job and have given up hope on pursuing the very dreams they are so passionate about. It is so sad and unnecessary.

Everyone Should Know ...
Debt can affect personal relationships.

Have you ever owed money to a family member? Even small amounts of borrowed money can create strife. I have seen entire families torn apart because of money and debt. There is a way to avoid that – avoid debt – especially debt owed to family members.

Everyone Should Know ...
Debt-free equals freedom.

When Jenn and I became highly focused on paying off all our debt in December 2002, we really had no idea how much we owed. After totaling it up, we realized we owed more than $15,000, and we were making debt payments of $755 every month.

When I saw that $755 was leaving my paycheck every single month to pay debt, I was outraged; I was frustrated; I was mad! I had no one to blame but myself. Our poor decisions led to the debt. We were going to have to deal with those decisions to break free, and we did.

We finished paying off all of our non-house debt in February 2004. It has been outstanding to live without a car, credit card, student loan, truck, engagement ring, wedding ring, or furniture payment!

We were then able to save, give away, and spend the $755 that was going to the banks every single month. We felt like millionaires because we had more than $4.13 in the bank account for the first time ever. This has provided so much freedom.

We did not realize the stress that our debt was creating until we paid it all off. Debt freedom brought so much relief because we were able to build a huge safety cushion in our finances. The days of panicking when the car broke down (and your car WILL break down) are gone. We have waved goodbye to the days where the dryer breaks down, and we have no idea how to pay for its repair or replacement.

It all equals freedom. Freedom to pursue what we have been put on earth to do. Freedom to pursue a life-giving crusade that pays less money. Freedom for Jenn to be a stay-at-home mom. Freedom to consider how we might bless others with financial gifts. Freedom to pursue our plans, hopes and dreams.

I have tried living life with a pile of debt, and I have lived a life free of debt. I like the debt-free life much better.

Everyone Should Know ...
Credit cards can be easily misused.

Credit cards are debt waiting to happen. A credit card allows one to make impulsive decisions without any barriers to prevent them. Once you have a credit card, you do not have to ask anyone for a loan. You do not have to fill out an application stating why you want to use it each time. There is no immediate accountability. This can result in financial disaster. I personally exited college with thousands of dollars in credit card debt.

I knew credit card debt was not good, yet I still used the card to purchase stuff. I justified the purchases by saying that I was going to earn enough money in the future to pay it off. This was true, but I failed to recognize that I was robbing myself of future giving, saving and spending.

I used a credit card to buy a ton of stuff, and I did not pay it off every single month. This happened because I did not have a written plan. I did not take fifteen minutes a month to think through the best use of my money. As a result, I would arrive at the end of the month having overspent my money. I chose to give in to my impulsive nature and used my credit cards to fund my wants.

Everyone Should Know ...
Debt can be wisely used.

Debt can be used wisely. Yes. It is true. I believe I have used debt wisely two different times – to obtain my engineering degree from Purdue University and to purchase my home. The student loan was certainly no fun to pay back, but it allowed me to focus on my education, obtain a fantastic degree, and graduate in four years. Student loans will be discussed in much more detail later, but there are two important points to understand here. First, I obtained a degree that would allow me to produce an income that let me easily pay back the student loan debt. Secondly, I finished in four years. This limited my student loan debt to the minimum amount necessary which helped me pay off my student loan debt earlier than most.

I used debt to purchase my home. My first home purchase cost $115,900. I will never forget signing the line to borrow six-figure debt. I borrowed money because I did not have $115,900 lying around as spare change. Most people do not. I made sure I was able to make at least a 5 percent down payment, had an excellent credit score, and that the house would sell for more than the purchase price. In other words, I did not purchase a house in a neighborhood with over-inflated home prices.

I sold that house three years later for $126,500. Since that time, I have bought and sold three houses. My wife and I have been blessed and now own a substantial portion of our current house and are on track to pay it off way early.

Debt can be used wisely when used to purchase items that go up in value and when entered into extremely cautiously with substantial financial margin to protect against loss.

Chapter SIX

Student Loans

Everyone Should Know ...
Student loans can crush your finances.

If you are in college or preparing for college and you are using or going to be using student loans to fund that education, I want you to ask yourself the following question.

Is the college degree worth the cost?

I ask this question because I have met many college students who have not asked it. There is a perception that a college degree is a ticket to the high life with great income and it justifies obtaining a degree at any cost. I disagree completely.

If the college degree is the equivalent of a degree in underwater basket weaving and the student ends up paying $40,000 for that degree, was it worth it? Probably not.

Everyone Should Know ...
Avoid student loans if at all possible.

What scholarship options are available to you? Apply for all of them. I obtained a scholarship from a sorority simply because I believe I was the only one to apply for it. Even small scholarships add up. They spend just like money.

I have seen students turn down a full-ride scholarship to attend another school that they liked more even though that school did not offer a full-ride. I cannot understand this logic. I know that some schools are "cooler" and "nicer" and "fancier" and carry more recognition, but I have to tell you that most people do not care where your degree came from.

I have a Bachelor of Science in Mechanical Engineering from Purdue University and a Masters of Business Administration from Clemson University. The companies I worked for could care less where my engineering and MBA degrees were from. They just wanted to know that I had earned them and that I was willing and able to apply that education.

As a business leader, I have personally discovered that I care a lot more about the individual effort a person has put forth into obtaining their degree than the school they attended.

Here is the approach I took toward student loans for my college education. I was the youngest of six boys, and my twin brother and I were the first ones in our family to go straight to college out of high school. It was up to me to fund my education, so I chose to attend a state school. It was a great school, and it was cheaper than a private school. I focused on obtaining a degree I knew would allow me to produce an income that would enable me to repay any student loans that I obtained.

When I graduated from Purdue, I had nearly $20,000 of student loans. Research had shown me that the average starting salary of a mechanical engineer was $37,000. I knew I would have the resources to pay back the loan, but it was still difficult to write that check every month. I had a 10-year student loan repayment schedule. Many people I meet with now have 20-year loan repayment schedules. This is a lot of time and money to pledge away for a college degree.

I paid my student loans off 1.5 years early, but it still took me 8.5 years. What else could I have done with that money? If I could go back and change my decision to obtain student loans, I am convinced that I would have worked more during the school year to minimize the amount of student loan debt I graduated with.

Everyone Should Know …
Attend college for four years for a four-year degree.

I cannot believe the number of students who end up taking five, six or even seven years to graduate with a four-year degree. I know college is a blast, but there is a tremendous cost to be paid for this type of delay.

What is the cost of going to school for two extra years? There is the cost of two additional years of school – tuition, room and board, books and fees. But the hidden cost that many do not recognize is the fact that two years of pay have been forfeited. Not only will the student have to pay for two extra years of school, but the student missed out on earning two years of income.

If I had taken two extra years to graduate from college, the opportunity cost would have been more than $80,000! Buckle down, study and earn a degree that allows you to fund your plans, hopes and dreams, and complete the degree on time.

You can even take summer school and graduate earlier than scheduled. This can allow you to do what you are called to do even earlier.

Everyone Should Know …
Consider attending a technical school for the first two years.

Attending a technical school for the first two years can be an extremely economical option for someone who has no money for college. It might even make sense to attend the technical school or community college for all four years.

Technical schools have vastly improved their capabilities and instructional faculty and are much cheaper than most universities. Attending a technical school for the first couple of years might not be glamorous, but neither is a pile of debt.

Everyone Should Know ...
You can work while attending college.

This might not be a great option for you, but many students work their way through college. I obtained my MBA while working a full-time job, becoming a father for the first time and trying to be a good husband. It was hard work, and it was much less exciting than when I obtained my undergraduate degree.

I was, however, able to graduate with a master's degree without incurring any new debt! It was certainly not as fun as my undergraduate degree, but it was outstanding to graduate knowing that I had no new debt while enhancing my earning power.

Chapter SEVEN

Credit Scores

Everyone Should Know ...
Your credit score will have an impact on your life.

Credit scores are a measure of one's ability to manage debt. The dominant credit scoring system which is used by most lenders was created by Fair Isaac. This system provides a measure of an individual's credit worthiness and is commonly known as a FICO Score.

A credit score impacts many things. It determines whether or not you can obtain a loan. If you qualify for a loan, the credit score dictates the interest rate charged.

Credit scores also impact insurability. When you obtain auto, renter's or homeowner's insurance, the credit score directly impacts the insurance cost. The lower your credit score, the higher the insurance premium will cost. I have seen insurance premiums doubled because of poor credit.

Credit scores also impact the ability to obtain a cell phone contract or an apartment lease. It can affect utility connections. Utility providers usually require much larger deposits from people who have low credit scores. If you have an excellent credit score, a deposit might be waived entirely. Credit scores can even impact your ability to obtain a job.

Everyone Should Know ...
The key measurements that determine a credit score.

The credit reporting agencies are secretive as to how they calculate credit scores, but it is well known that credit scores are directly impacted by the following items:

- Type of credit issued
  - Revolving debt (credit card)
  - Installment debt (anything with payments and a pay-off – car loan, boat loan, student loan, etc.)
- Age of the credit relationship
- Amount of credit one can obtain (total of all credit limits)
- Amount of credit one has consumed (percentage of total credit limit)
- Payment timeliness
- Requests for credit
- Outstanding judgments

According to FICO's publication, *Understanding Your FICO Score*, a FICO credit score is determined in the following way for the general population.

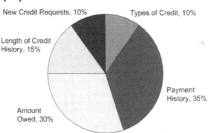

FICO scoring breakdown [from FICO's publication, *Understanding Your Credit Score*]

For people who are just establishing credit, it will be different since payment history is not yet available.

Everyone Should Know ...
How to establish a credit history and build a great credit score.

Many young people ask me, "How do I even get a credit score?" They have no credit history, which makes it difficult to obtain credit, so it appears they are in a tough no-win situation.

Here are some ways to establish credit. Obtain a credit card from a local department store. Plan to spend a certain amount at that store using a written spending plan. Purchase the item at the store using the credit card. As soon as the credit card transaction is completed, tell the checkout clerk that you want to make a credit card payment. Immediately pay off the credit card. Making purchases like this once or twice each month can really lead to a great credit score.

This impacts the credit score in several positive ways. The age of the credit relationship increases. Payment timeliness receives another good mark. Over time, the credit card issuer will most likely increase the credit limit because they will see that you have managed your smaller credit limit well. As a result, your "percent of available credit utilized" will decrease. This bodes well for your FICO score.

If you do not qualify for an unsecured credit card, you can apply for a secured credit card. A secured credit card works in the following manner. The credit card company requires you to have money in an account that they provide. The credit card company prevents your use of this money by placing it on hold. If you fail to pay the credit card payments, the credit card company will use these funds to satisfy the debt.

I must issue a strong warning. NONE of these credit-building techniques will work well financially if you do not apply the rest of the learnings in this book. If you obtain a credit card, run up a balance, fail to pay it off immediately, and end up paying compound interest to the bank. You might end up with a great credit score, but you will be losing financially.

I have met many people who have an OUTSTANDING credit score, but they are flat broke. They have financed themselves to oblivion, but have managed to pay their payments on time. One minor event can lead to financial ruin for these individuals, and I have seen this happen hundreds of times.

Everyone Should Know ...
What number is a good credit score?

According to Fair Isaac, a credit score can range from 300 to 850. The higher the score, the lower the risk. This means you want a higher number.

Companies establish their own criteria as to which credit score is a good credit score. As a general rule, any FICO score greater than 750 is an excellent credit score. Anything more than 800 is considered outstanding. As credit scores drift into the 600 range, credit might still be available, but it will come at a higher cost. Credit scores in the 500 range might prevent you from obtaining reasonable lending rates and terms.

Everyone Should Know ...
A credit score is a debt management score, not a measure of your financial health.

Review the items that comprise a FICO score. Did you notice that it does not include items such as:
o The amount of money in a savings/checking or retirement account?
o The amount of equity in a home?
o Paid-for items that have value (car, house, expensive jewelry, etc.)

A FICO credit score only looks at debt. One could literally have $1 million in the bank and have a credit score of ZERO because they have not used debt for a long period of time.

There are people who define themselves by their credit score. "My credit score is 801," they boast. I have seen many people who have extremely high credit scores who are absolutely broke. They have a high credit score because they have managed their debt well, not because they have managed their money well!

There are many people who have purchased a brand new car using debt when they could have paid cash for a nice used car. They bought the new car solely to boost their credit score. It might improve their credit score, but it hurts them where it really counts – the bank account!

Everyone Should Know ...
How to maintain a great credit score.

Go back to the section that details the key items that determine your credit score and do those items well. Pay your bills on time. Pay credit cards off every month. Limit your inquiries for credit. Avoid judgments against you. Maintain long-term relationships with your credit issuers.

It is important to obtain your credit report at least once a year. You are allowed to receive a free credit report once each year from each of the three credit reporting agencies – TransUnion, Experian and Equifax. You can do so FREE by visiting www.annualcreditreport.com.

Even if you have a good credit score, you should make it a habit to check your credit report at least once a year because errors do happen. With the impact that a credit score has on one's life, it is important to know that your credit report is 100 percent correct.

Your credit score should not define who you are, but it will play an important role in your future financial decisions.

Chapter EIGHT

Compound Interest

Everyone Should Know ...
Compound interest is REAL and AMAZING.

Compound interest has the ability to radically change your life – for better or for worse. It has the ability to help you fund your life's plans, hopes and dreams. It can rob you of your plans, hopes and dreams. It has incredible power. The good news is that you have the ability to determine whether it will help you or hinder you. It is real and amazing.

Everyone Should Know ...
How interest works.

It is extremely important to understand how compound interest works. I will start by explaining the word "interest." Interest is money that is paid to you because you have loaned your money to someone else.

For example, when you place money into a savings account at the bank, you are really loaning that money to the bank. The bank will pay you "interest" for the loan. The interest rate varies from 0.10 percent to nearly 5 percent per year. If you have $200 dollars in a savings account at the bank for a year and the bank pays 3 percent interest, then the bank will add six dollars to your account ($200 x 3% = $6).

Think about that for one moment. You are given money simply because you have money! You did not work for that money. You did not sweat for that money. You simply left the two hundred dollars in the savings account, and the bank gave you $6. I told you it is real and amazing!

Everyone Should Know ...
How compound interest works.

Compound interest is simply the payment of interest over time. Let us pick up the example of $200 in the savings account that was paid interest of $6 after one year.

Suppose that the $206 is left alone for the next year. Will you be paid another $6? No – because you will be paid 3% interest on the $206. Instead of being paid six dollars, you will be given $6.18.

This is how compound interest works. As one is paid interest, the account balance grows and more interest must be paid to you! The borrower (the bank) must pay you interest on the interest they have already paid to you. If you have patience, compound interest becomes a runaway freight train. Check out how much the $200 grows over 50 years.

| $200 receiving 3% annual interest ||
Years	Value
10	$270
20	$364
30	$491
40	$663
50	$895

- 42 -

The $200 grows to over four times more. This is good, but look what happens if you are paid even higher interest during that 50 year period.

At different annual interest rates, $200 grows into ...					
Years	**3%**	**6%**	**8%**	**10%**	**12%**
10	$270	$363	$443	$541	$660
20	$364	$662	$985	$1,465	$2,178
30	$491	$1,204	$2,187	$3,967	$7,189
40	$663	$2,191	$4,854	$10,740	$23,729
50	$895	$3,987	$10,775	$29,073	$78,316

Do you see the number in the 12% box? The $200 turns into $78,316. The number is almost unbelievable, but it is real. I have personally seen it work in my own life.

The cost of spending $200 on a new wardrobe is $78,316 if you were able to receive 12 percent interest on the same $200 for 50 years. I certainly do not save every single dollar I earn, but this fact has caused me to maximize the amount of money I save because it will fund my future plans, hopes and dreams. Compound interest can help me achieve far more than I ever thought possible.

Now, it can be really hard to believe that $200 can become $78,316 if it grows at 12 percent each year for 50 years, so I want to show you how this works in detail to ensure that you clearly understand how compound interest works.

Look at the interest that the $200 earns in the first month of the investment.

Year	Month	Value	Interest Gain	New Value
1	1	$200	$2	202

The 12 percent interest is **annual** growth. Interest is commonly referred to in annual amounts. Since this interest was paid for one month, one-twelfth (I percent) of the interest was paid out. One percent of $200 is $2.

Now let us look at month number two. Instead of receiving interest on just the $200, we will now receive interest on the $200 *plus* the $2 interest we were paid last month. This is where the "compound" portion of "compound interest" comes into play!

Year	Month	Value	Interest Gain	New Value
1	2	$202	$2.02	$204.02

We were given $2.02 in interest this month. While the two pennies are seemingly very small, they are vitally important to the wild growth of this investment later. On to month three.

Year	Month	Value	Interest Gain	New Value
1	3	$204.02	$2.04	$206.06

The interest has grown to $2.04.

Now let's look at the end of the first year.

Year	Month	Value	Interest Gain	New Value
1	12	$223.14	$2.23	$225.37

The monthly interest gained has now grown to $2.23 and the $200 investment has now grown by $25.37.

Now check out the calculations as the investment continues for 50 years.

$200 initial investment – 12% annual interest				
Year	Month	Value	Interest Gain	New Value
1	1	$200	$2.00	$202
1	2	$202	$2.02	$204.02
1	3	$204.02	$2.04	$206.06
1	12	$223.14	$2.23	$225.37
5	12	$359.74	$3.60	$363.34
10	12	$653.54	$6.54	$660.08
20	12	$2,156.94	$21.57	$2,178.51
30	12	$7,118.74	$71.19	$7,189.93
40	12	$23,494.60	$234.95	$23,729.55
50	12	$77,541.27	$775.41	$78,316.68

It is amazing to watch compound interest calculations on paper. It is even more amazing to watch it happen with real money in real investments. I am a living witness to the power of compound interest.

Everyone Should Know ...
Compound interest can work against you!

It is astonishing to watch how compound interest can work FOR someone, but it can also work AGAINST someone. The same power of compound interest works against someone when they sign up for debt and agree to pay interest on the loan or if the purchase drops in value from day one. The same compound interest that could have helped fund plans, hopes and dreams will instead rob them.

For example, suppose someone wanted a new TV, but they did not have the money to pay for it. Instead, they financed it on a department store credit card. A $1,000 purchase price using a credit card with a 21.99 percent interest rate.

The minimum payment of 2 percent of the original loan is $20. It will take 11 years and six months to pay it off. The total payments will be $2,740 for an original loan of $1,000. Compound interest totaling $1,740 was paid directly to the bank for the convenience of obtaining the money immediately. This is what I call a negative net worth transaction!

Now, of course, almost no one intends to pay only minimum payments when they obtain debt, but I see it all the time. Reality reveals that many people have financed themselves into a terrible financial situation, and compound interest is battering their lives.

You have a choice. You can have compound interest work for you, or you can have it working against you. Choose to have it work FOR you!

Everyone Should Know ...
Risk helps determine the amount of interest received.

The amount of interest received is dependent upon the risk that has been taken with the money. If your money is placed in a FDIC-insured savings account at the bank, there has been almost no risk taken with that money. This means that the interest rate will be extremely low. Usually it will be below the rate of inflation – the rate at which ordinary goods and services increase in cost. No risk equals lower interest.

If your money is used to purchase a company stock, there is substantially higher risk. If the company fails to make a profit and declares bankruptcy, the stock value could drop to zero. However, if the company makes a profit, it could decide to pay you (the stockholder) some of those profits. Also, if the company grows in value, the stock price can increase. There are no guarantees. This means there is more risk. If you are willing to take more risk, there is a greater chance of growth and loss. In the next section I will show you why I am willing to take the risk.

Everyone Should Know ...
Time, amount invested and interest greatly affect investment growth.

When it comes to compound interest, there are three very important factors – time, amount invested and the interest received. All three matter – a lot!

Time

Time matters a lot. Look at the $200 compound interest example. If you would have waited 10 years to invest the $200, the difference at the 50 year mark would be $54,587.13. Just for waiting 10 years. Time matters – a lot!

Amount Invested

The amount invested matters a lot. If you would have invested $50 instead of $200, you would have only $19,579.17. A difference of $58,737.51. The amount invested matters – a lot!

Interest Received

The interest received matters just as much as the time and amount invested. In the $200 compound interest example, we looked at an interest rate of 12 percent per year. If one were to have left the money in a FDIC-insured savings account that paid 4 percent per year, the $200 would have grown to $1,472.90. A difference of $76,843.78. The interest rate received matters – a lot!

Everyone Should Know ...
Invest every month for the rest of your life.

We have seen that the time, amount invested, and interest received matter a lot. It is now important to look at another example where one invests $50 every single month for the next 50 years. If we assume that the investment will grow at 12 percent per year, then the investment will grow to

$1,952,917 in 50 years! For 50 bucks, one can have nearly $2 million! What if I am wrong and you only achieve half of this amount? Are you going to call me up and be angry with me? I will be happy to take that call!

Invest $50/month – 12% annual interest		
Year	Month	Value
5	12	$4,083
10	12	$11,502
15	12	$24,979
20	12	$49,463
25	12	$93,942
30	12	$174,748
35	12	$321,548
40	12	$588,239
45	12	$1,072,735
50	12	$1,952,917

For some reason, people are captivated by the seven-figure number $1,000,000. This amount of wealth is achievable, and of course it takes time, excellent growth and regular investing to achieve. Below is a chart that shows you how long it will take different monthly investments to reach $1,000,000 at different annual interest rates.

Years to reach $1,000,000					
Monthly Amount	6%	8%	10%	12%	14%
$25	88.6	70.1	58.4	50.2	44.2
$50	77.1	61.5	51.4	44.4	39.2
$100	65.7	52.9	44.5	38.7	34.3
$250	50.9	41.6	35.5	31.1	27.8
$500	40.1	33.4	28.8	25.5	22.9
$1,000	29.9	25.5	22.4	20.1	18.2

This example shows the absolute importance of consistent investing and obtaining a good return on investment. I have found no investments that have paid 12 percent every single year, but I have found several mutual funds that have returned an average of more than 12 percent for the past 50-plus years. There are years where the mutual fund lost 15 percent. There are also years where the mutual fund grew over 30 percent!

Control what you can control – invest every single month for your entire life. It will provide you with a ton of money to give away to your family and to causes you really believe in!

Everyone Should Know ...
Invested money is money not needed for at least five years.

I have a personal rule that I will not invest money that I will need to use within the next five years. If I believe that I will need the money within the next five years, that money is placed in secure, FDIC-insured savings accounts. I do this because I want to make sure that the money will be available and because many investments go up and down in value over the short term. I do not want to risk losing the money I know I will need within the next five years.

What do I do with the rest of the money I have planned to invest? I invest it in stocks, mutual funds, small business and real estate. I love investing money because it helps me fund my future hopes, plans and dreams!

Everyone Should Know ...
Always consider risk and diversification.

We have already discussed that risk impacts the potential return or loss on an investment. In general, the higher the risk, the higher the opportunity for a larger gain or loss.

Consider two commonly known "investments" – the lottery and a FDIC-insured bank savings account. The lottery "investment" (investment being used **very** loosely) has super high risk because there is a small chance for a huge return and a high chance for a 100 percent loss. This huge risk is why the winner receives such a huge pay out for their "investment."

An "investment" into a FDIC-insured bank savings account has very little risk. If the bank fails, the money is insured by the United States government. The money has extremely low risk, so banks pay extremely low interest on that investment.

Another key to investing is to have excellent diversification. Diversification simply means that your money is spread into separate investments. For example, someone might have their investments diversified into stock mutual funds, bank certificate of deposits and real estate.

Diversification is very important because it helps protect against losing all of the invested money. Consider an example where a person had all of their investments in one single company stock. If the company declared bankruptcy, the individual could lose absolutely everything. This would be awful, and unfortunately, it has happened to countless people through the ages.

Recent examples include MCI-WorldCom and Enron. There were literally thousands of people who lost their life savings because they neglected the importance of a diversified portfolio.

Everyone Should Know ...
Mutual funds provide instant diversification.

A mutual fund is a collection of company stocks, bonds and other investments that are purchased by a mutual fund team. The mutual fund company obtains the money to purchase the investments from investors like you and me.

We all "mutually" send "funds" to the mutual fund company, and they use the money to purchase investments. We have "mutually funded" the investment. This is how the word "Mutual Fund" evolved.

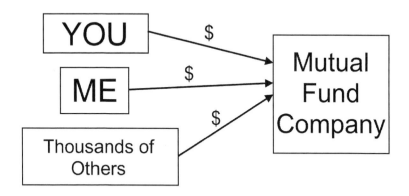

I am a huge fan of mutual funds because they provide instant diversification and reduce risk. Each mutual fund has a specific objective. Some invest only in American companies. Others focus investments solely in emerging countries. Some even focus on specific industries or technologies.

You can learn a lot more about mutual funds by visiting an investment advisor or by visiting Morningstar.com, a great web site focused almost entirely on investing.

Everyone Should Know ...
Start investing as soon as possible!

Of the three most critical factors involved in ensuring that compound interest works FOR us, we can only control two of them completely. We can control the length of time we invest, and we can control the amount we invest. As a result, it is important to start investing right away.

Look at an example of Joe and John. Joe started investing $2,000 a year at age 20. He stopped investing additional money after 10 years. John started investing at age 40 and invested $10,000 per year all the way to age 65.

Example assumes 12% annual interest					
Age	Years	Joe [Total Invested]	John [Total Invested]	Joe [Value]	John [Value]
25	5	$10,000	$0	$12,706	$0
30	10	$20,000	$0	$35,097	$0
35	15	$20,000	$0	$61,854	$0
40	20	$20,000	$0	$109,007	$0
45	25	$20,000	$50,000	$192,108	$63,528
50	30	$20,000	$100,000	$338,560	$175,487
55	35	$20,000	$150,000	$596,659	$372,797
60	40	$20,000	$200,000	$1,051,517	$720,524
65	45	$20,000	$250,000	$1,853,133	$1,333,339

At age 65, Joe will have $519,794 more than John even though John has personally invested $230,000 more than Joe. This is why it is so essential to start investing as soon as possible.

You can begin investing immediately. I recommend that you find someone you trust who has won with their own money and ask them to help you. Be sure that this person will not try to sell you something or will personally benefit from the advice they give you as this can create a conflict of interest.

The primary goal of any investment is to make money. The secondary goal is to shield the investment growth from taxation since taxes can substantially erode the impact of compound interest. There are many tax-advantaged investing options available. A company 401(k) is one such option. Roth IRAs and Traditional IRAs are other options.

As soon as you are employed full-time, your employer will most likely have a retirement plan available. It could be called a 401(k), 403(b), 457 or Thrift Savings Plan. If the employer matches a portion of your investment, this is **FREE** money. Be sure to invest enough to at least obtain all of the employer match.

To retire well, invest at least 10 percent of your gross income. If you want to retire wealthy, invest at least 15 percent. You will never regret the decision to save and invest money!

Chapter NINE

Purchasing A Home

Everyone Should Know ...
"Gotta-Have-A-House Fever" is real.

Purchasing a house is exciting, scary, intimidating and thrilling – all at the same time. With all of these emotions happening at once, it is easy to become emotions-driven instead of logic-driven. For many, a home is symbolic of "making it" or "arriving." It defines who they are.

The "Gotta-Have-A-House Fever," however, can cause you to purchase a house that is way too expensive, in need of costly repairs that you cannot afford, or overpriced.

You have probably experienced similar emotions when purchasing other items, but buying a house is different because it costs so much and it is much more difficult to recover from a mistake.

You might have purchased a cell phone that you thought would be incredible, but it turned out to be a worthless paperweight. This situation would be very frustrating, but it is fixed relatively easily. You can toss the cell phone into a recycle bin and buy a new one. The financial and time costs are minimal. It is much different for a house. A house cannot be thrown into the recycle bin too easily, and selling it can be extremely difficult and time-consuming.

There is a huge chance that you will experience "Gotta-Have-A-House Fever." Here are steps you can take to deal with it.

1. Recognize that you have the "fever."
2. If married, communicate with your spouse that you are experiencing the "fever."
3. Before looking at homes, determine the maximum amount you are willing to pay for a house, write that number down, and hold yourself to it.
4. Save for a down payment – the time it takes to save it will help you realize the enormity of this purchase.
5. Establish accountability with someone who has purchased a few houses in his/her life – ask them to walk through this process with you.

Everyone Should Know ...
What to do before looking for a home.

Recognize "Gotta-Have-A-House Fever"

It has already been discussed that you must recognize that "Gotta-Have-A-House Fever" is real. Knowing this BEFORE looking for your home is very important.

Obtain Mortgage Pre-Approval

Mortgage pre-approval is a process where the lender reviews your financial situation and determines the amount that they are willing to lend you for a home purchase. This pre-approval is essential because it will set you apart from many potential buyers. When you are negotiating to purchase your house, the pre-approval allows the seller to know for sure that you are able to buy the house. I have personally accepted an offer because the purchaser provided proof that they had the money to complete the deal, and their offer was not subject to credit approval.

It is important to understand that just because a bank has approved you for a specific loan amount does not mean that it is a wise decision to borrow all of it. In fact, it is rarely a wise decision to borrow all of the approved amount. You can (and probably should) spend less than the approved amount so you can still have fun while owning the home. A general guideline is for the mortgage payment, including taxes and insurance, to not exceed 25 percent of take-home pay.

The most common mortgage repayment terms are for 30 years, but consider obtaining a 15-year mortgage or pay higher payments toward a 30-year loan as if it were a 15-year mortgage. The two key advantages of a 15-year mortgage over a 30-year note are (1) it will be paid off 15 years sooner and (2) 15-year notes tend to have a slightly lower interest rate. The disadvantage is that it will require a higher monthly payment.

Also consider obtaining a fixed rate mortgage. This means that the interest rate will not change during the loan's term. A fixed rate provides an assurance to you as a borrower that your payments will not vary.

A free mortgage payment calculator is available via the "Free Tools" link located at www.IWasBrokeNowImNot.com.

Consider Renting vs. Buying

Buying a house can be a great thing, but it also comes with limitations that are not immediately obvious – especially if you have a case of "Gotta-Have-A-House Fever."

Owning a home means that you have to fix the broken toilet and leaking faucet. You have to mow the lawn and maintain the landscaping. When the air conditioner or heater dies, you have the joy of paying for it. When the roof leaks, you have to pay for the patch or a new roof. If the stove breaks, guess who gets to pay for it? Property taxes and homeowner's insurance become part of life. A house is usually larger than a rental unit, and this means that the utilities will cost more as well. When you purchase a house, it also means it is more permanent. Selling a house can take a lot longer and cost more than breaking a lease.

Take the time to prepare a written list of pros and cons of renting and purchasing a home. NOTE: If you are preparing to purchase a house right now – and you feel resistant to the idea of preparing this list of pros and cons – you just might have a case of "Gotta-Have-A-House Fever!"

Save at least enough money for a 5 percent down payment

To qualify for a conventional mortgage with the best interest rates, a 5 percent down payment is usually required. The reason you are able to obtain lower interest rates with at least a 5 percent down payment is because this lowers the risk for the lender. The risk is lower because you are much less likely to stop paying for a house in which you have invested thousands of your own dollars.

A 5 percent down payment also allows one to avoid becoming upside-down (owing more than it is worth) on the house. When someone owes more on a house than it is worth, it is called "negative equity." Most people do not have the ability to market and sell their house on their own. A typical real estate commission is 5 to 7 percent of the selling price. If you purchased a house at retail price and did not make a down payment, the house is instantly in a negative equity position. If you should need to sell the house within the first few years, you will have to pay for the negative equity before ownership can be transferred to the buyer. Purchasing a house with 0 percent down and financing the entire transaction is a recipe for financial disaster.

A 5 percent down payment is great, but a 20 percent down payment is even better. If you do not own 20 percent of the home's value, the mortgage company will require you to purchase private mortgage insurance (PMI). This typically costs between $40 and $100 per month. This size of down payment is a monumental amount for most people, but it can allow you to save a ton of money on PMI. Another way to avoid PMI is to purchase a house at less than 80 percent of its value. These types of deals do exist, but they require patience and diligence to locate them.

Have an emergency fund of at least $2,500

This $2,500 is in addition to the 5 percent down payment. This is necessary because houses have the potential for large unexpected emergency expenses. An appliance will fail. A tree might fall on the garage. The septic system might need replacing. All of these cost money. If you purchase a house and use all of your available money just to make the down payment, you are at risk of incurring debt that is avoidable just by having an emergency fund. $2,500 is a starting point. A better number is $10,000.

Know what an "escrow account" is and how it operates

Many lenders require an escrow account when purchasing a home. An escrow account operates much like a savings account. When you pay your monthly payment, it will include money for the principal and interest of the mortgage loan plus an additional amount for the escrow account. This escrow money is saved in your account and is utilized to pay your homeowner's insurance premium and property taxes.

The reason that most lenders require an escrow account is because they have taken the majority of the risk. Suppose you purchased a home for $100,000 and made a $5,000 down payment. Your risk is the $5,000 down payment. The lender's risk is the $95,000 that was loaned to you. If you fail to pay your taxes or homeowner's insurance, the house could be lost for failure to pay taxes or a fire could occur without insurance. The escrow account reduces the risk of financial loss for both you and the lender.

Everyone Should Know ...

What to do when looking for a home to purchase.

Start on line

The Internet has outstanding resources for researching homes that are for sale. Zillow.com and Realtor.com are two excellent places to start. You can search using criteria specific to your wants and needs. Search options include the number of bedrooms, bathrooms, garage size, parking spot, dock or boat slip availability, land, location and many others. Most listings have pictures. Many have 360 degree views or videos. You can even see the listings placed on a map.

An on line search allows you to answer critical questions for your search:

- Do you have reasonable expectations for what you can afford to purchase?
- How many houses are available?
- What is the market price range?

The convenience of the Internet will allow you to view literally hundreds of options in the time that it might take to physically visit one or two houses. Leverage this outstanding information to narrow down your search to the houses that appeal to you the most.

Search for homes in the middle to lower price range

Homes priced at the upper end of the price range for an area generally have a more difficult time selling in a reasonable timeframe. By purchasing a home that is priced in the middle to lower price range for the area, you will maximize the potential return on your investment.

In general, homes that are priced in the middle to lower price range will (when compared to houses priced in the upper end of the price range) sell faster, obtain a better rate of return on investment and have a larger number of potential purchasers.

Work with a real-estate agent who is highly effective

A highly effective real-estate agent can be quickly identified. They are the ones who sell the most houses every year. I have found out that there is a great reason for their high sales numbers – they are really good at what they do! They know how to match up homes with your desires, and they will ensure that your questions will be answered promptly.

Many agents will attempt to have you sign an "exclusive" agreement to work only with them as you search for a home. I have never signed one because I have always wanted the option of working with another agent. Great real estate agents also know how to negotiate and can help you navigate the mountains of paperwork associated with purchasing your first home.

Know your limits and boundaries

Do you like tearing apart a house and completely remodeling it? If not, you should avoid purchasing a "fixer-upper." Remodeling consumes a lot of time and money.

Establish non-negotiables that are deal-breakers if they are not met. For example, I always want an attached garage as part of my home. If I see a great home without an attached garage, it is a deal-breaker. Some common non-negotiables are the number of bedrooms, number of bathrooms, lot size, location, school district and years-since-built.

Visiting homes

Once you have narrowed your focus on a few houses, it is time to visit them. This is very exciting and can be emotional. Be sure to keep the "Gotta-Have-A-House Fever" in check.

As you prepare to visit, prepare a written checklist of the different items that are non-negotiables so you can check them off as you see them. You also might want to provide a rating scale for the data.

Bring a digital camera with you to take pictures of each house as you visit them. This can be an extremely helpful tool to remember each house since you will be visiting several of them, and certain details could be forgotten.

Deciding which house to purchase

This is an emotional decision because a house means more than just spending an enormous amount of money. It is where you will spend a lot of time, energy and effort. Your friends and family will be visiting you there.

Narrow down the list to your favorite houses that remain as an option and then prepare a list of positive and negative characteristics of each one. When I have purchased homes, I have listed the non-negotiables at the top of my list to help ensure that I did not make a purchase that violated these boundaries.

If none of the houses meet your reasonable expectations, start over! It may be disheartening to go back to the start, but there are millions of houses on the planet, and it is more important to know you have made a great decision.

Everyone Should Know ...

What to do when negotiating to purchase a home.

Everything is negotiable

Once you have decided on a home to purchase, it is time to negotiate. This can be an intimidating process, but it does not have to be. A great real estate agent is extremely helpful in this case. It is also important to seek wisdom from others you trust.

What is negotiable? Price, repairs, furniture, lawn mowers, appliances, curtains, closing costs and home warranties. There are many more, but these are some very common ones. Your requests must be written down in contract form to legally bind the agreement.

The purchase contract should include ...

The purchase contract should include everything that was negotiated. If you negotiated that the stove, refrigerator, curtains and lawn mower would be included with the purchase, this must be documented.

The contract should include a requirement that the sale is subject to financing approval. Even if you have obtained pre-approval for a mortgage, you still want to include this requirement just in case something happens during the closing process and your loan is refused or delayed.

Include a requirement that the home must pass a home inspection by a certified inspector. A certified inspector is trained to look at each system in your entire house for overall condition. This includes an inspection of the foundation, construction, electrical system, plumbing, heating/cooling units, lighting, carpet, flooring, attic, roof and a review of the property. I have found the home inspection to be absolutely essential in the purchase of the four homes I have bought.

Also include a requirement that the purchase is subject to an appraisal that equals or exceeds the purchase price. An appraisal is completed by a third party to ensure that the home is worth the agreed upon amount. This protects you and the lender from making a negative equity purchase.

All agreed-upon items are to be included in the contract. Word of mouth will not stand up in court very well. If an agreement has been made, have it written into the contract, sign it and ensure the seller has signed it as well. A signed purchase agreement means that if all stipulations included within the contract are satisfied, you will soon be owning a home!

It is common practice for a small deposit be made with a purchase offer. This is called earnest money. It communicates to the purchaser that you are serious about purchasing the house. If a purchase agreement is not reached, you will generally receive the money back. There are exceptions to this, however, so it is important to make a small earnest money deposit. If the deal progresses to closing, and you indeed purchase the home, the earnest money becomes part of your down payment.

Once you have an agreement, contact your mortgage lender and provide them the contract. This will start the process toward finalizing the purchase. Your lender will provide you a Good Faith Estimate that will help you understand the costs associated with the purchase.

Everyone Should Know ...
What happens when finalizing the purchase.

The process has been time-consuming. You have prepared to purchase a house by saving money, determined the amount of money to save for a down payment, and calculated the monthly payment you can manage well. You have obtained mortgage pre-approval, looked at hundreds of houses, and selected a house. The negotiations have taken place, and a contract has been written. All of the details have been completed, and now THE DAY has finally arrived.

A great real estate agent should prepare you well for this day. By law, you will be given a HUD Statement. The HUD Statement is similar to the Good Faith Estimate except this document will clearly detail the actual expenses associated with the purchase of the home – including the closing costs and the down payment you are required to bring with you to the closing meeting.

An attorney might be present at the closing meeting. I have always had one present when closing on my real estate purchases. The real estate attorney, or individual who is overseeing the closing, will go through each document page by page and answer any questions you might have.

Once all of your questions are answered to your satisfaction, it is time to sign the documents. Expect to sign your name at least 30 times. When all the documents are completed and you have made the appropriate payments, you will be the proud owner of your new home. Congratulations!

Chapter TEN

Insurance

Everyone Should Know ...
Insurance protects and transfers risk.

There are so many types of insurance. The wide variety of options can make insurance a very confusing product to understand, and it can be difficult to know if you are making wise decisions. You can make great choices by asking questions, being informed and always understanding how each policy works before you purchase it.

I carry auto insurance because I drive a vehicle. It moves around. I have a high chance that I might run into something. The insurance allows me to transfer the risk to someone else. I also ensure that I pay attention when I drive, and I keep speeding to a minimum. This allows me to have the best insurance rates. Another good reason to have auto insurance is that the government mandates that I have it if I want to drive.

I have home insurance because I own a home. It does not move around, but it could be hit by a tree or burn down. To transfer the risk to someone else, I purchased homeowner's insurance. When I rented an apartment, I carried renter's insurance.

I have health insurance because with a 100 percent mortality rate, I assume that I or someone in my family will be sick some day. Health insurance transfers the risk to someone else – the insurance company.

I carry disability insurance to protect my family against the loss of my income should I become physically unable to work and produce income.

I have obtained life insurance to replace my income should I die prematurely. I carry term life insurance, which is much cheaper than whole life insurance. I hold a 30-year life insurance policy that will protect me all the way to retirement. Because I will have no debt and will have leveraged compound interest to work for me for the entire 30-year period, I plan to be self-insured when my policy expires.

Those are the only types of insurance I have purchased. Your needs might be different. When it comes to insurance, I keep it simple and seek to transfer risk.

Some have chosen to not carry insurance. It is their choice, but I have met hundreds (if not thousands) of people who have been destroyed by the lack of insurance. More than half of the bankruptcies filed in the United States are because of medical bills that resulted from not having no or inadequate insurance.

How terrible would it be to do all of the right things like planning your spending, saving every month, giving a bunch away and leveraging the power of compound interest only to lose it all when one major health incident or job loss occurred? Insurance is expensive, but it is far less expensive than not having insurance at all.

Chapter ELEVEN

Relationships

Everyone Should Know ...
Money affects relationships.

I am sure you are stunned by the news that money affects relationships. It is not news to anyone, yet I have met with a lot of people who are blind to the impact their money decisions are having on their relationships. Money affects relationships!

I have met with many parents who are not speaking to their son or daughter because they believe that the son or daughter has wronged them financially. The parents loaned money to their son, and the son has failed to repay the money. My heart hurts for them both.

Consider an example where the parents loaned their son $20,000 dollars because he was in a financial mess. A couple of years have passed, and the son has failed to repay the money. Now the relationship between the parents and the son is strained.

If I were to ask the parents, "Was it worth $20,000 to lose your relationship with your son?" most parents would respond saying they wish they would have just given him the money. If I were to ask the son, "Was it worth $20,000 to jeopardize the relationship with your parents?" most sons would respond, "Absolutely not."

I have also seen parents fail to repay their daughter who loaned them money. Same sad story. It was simply not worth it.

I have seen relationship issues happen between siblings. One sibling loans money to another and before you know it, there is a complete mess on everyone's hands. One sister talks about the other sister's no-count husband, and an all-out family feud breaks out. The cons far outweigh the benefits when it comes to loaning money to family members.

Because of the relationships I have seen messed up by loans made to family members, I will never borrow money from a family member. Nor will I ever loan money to a family member.

The solution? GIVE the money away. If someone in your family needs help, give them the money. I have given money to help family members, and all I require is a written EZ™ spending plan for the money. I attempt to teach them a financial principle as I bless them with the financial gift.

Giving the money away allows you to bless the family member, allows them to keep their dignity and prevents the relationship fiasco that usually ensues with a loan.

Everyone Should Know ...
Money affects marriages.

If you are married, you already know this. If you are not married, but plan to marry some day, consider this next thought. Your financial situation when you say, "I do," will have an impact on your marriage. If you have managed your money well, have saved money and are 100 percent debt-free, you are positioning yourself to have limited fights about money. If you have managed to finance everything you have, are barely able to pay your bills and have debt collectors calling you every day, you are setting yourself up for marriage troubles.

They say that the number one thing couples fight about is money. If that is true, it should be worth it to you to make every effort to enter marriage in the best financial condition possible.

I brought a ton of debt into marriage. My bride brought debts totaling less than $2,000. It took us six years to arrive on the same page financially. Once we prepared a written spending plan and began agreeing on where our money should go, we have had very few money fights. When we do, it is usually about which dream will be funded next. Those are great discussions!

Of course, an entire book could be written (and several have been) about relationships and the impact that money can have. I will not attempt to tackle all of the complex issues related to this subject, but here are some things that have worked well for Jenn and me.

- We prepare a written spending plan every month.
- We agree on a written spending plan before it is finalized.
- We walk away from the plan for a while to think about it some more if there is a disagreement.
- We agreed to never make a major purchase without the other one knowing about it in advance.
- We also have agreed to wait at least one day before making a large purchase.
- We regularly talk about our plans, hopes and dreams.
- We ensure that our plans, hopes and dreams are being funded every single month.
- We have agreed to use cash envelopes for "tend-to-be-impulsive" purchase categories to avoid overspending.

Chapter TWELVE

Discipline

Everyone Should Know ...
It is all about discipline.

Since you have made it to this page, you have already learned about or have been reminded of great financial knowledge. Now what are you going to do with all of this information?

I heard my friend, Perry Noble, once say, "We have already been educated way beyond our level of obedience." This is so true. Many times I *know* what I *should* do, but for some reason I do not do it.

The key is discipline. Discipline ensures that you not only prepare a written spending plan, but actually follow it. Discipline causes you to not only recognize that the car will break down someday, but also to save money to repair or replace it. I included this chapter to provide some practical tips that will help you maintain the discipline to develop your own financial plan and stick to it.

Everyone Should Know ...

Know where the money goes.

It is incredibly important to know where your money goes. You do not have to be a financial nerd to track where your money goes. I started out by keeping a basic hand-written check register given to me by the bank when I opened an account. I now use Microsoft Money. Others use Quicken. Many others use a free on line tool like Mint.com. It is simple to track where the money goes. It only requires discipline and a few minutes every month. One simply writes down all transactions for that period of time including both deposits and withdrawals.

I like using Microsoft Money because it allows me to categorize the income and expenses. I am able to see how much money I have spent on clothing, gasoline, insurance, food and entertainment for a set period of time.

It is important to keep track of where the money goes because you can:

- See where the majority is spent
- Identify potential opportunities for saving money
- Ensure you do not overspend your bank account which would result in extraordinary fees and charges
- Compare your actual spending versus the EZ spending plan that you prepared for that particular month
- Use your records to refer to past expenses which will help you prepare for future expenses (I look at last year's spending plan when preparing the spending plan for this year)

Develop the habit of tracking your spending. It will help you become a much better money manager, and since you are going to win big time, this will be a very helpful skill set!

Everyone Should Know ...
Always consider opportunity cost.

Opportunity cost is an economics term used to describe the next best alternative use of money. Suppose you have $100 and are choosing between attending a concert or shopping. If you choose to go to the concert, then your opportunity cost is shopping. You have given up the opportunity to go shopping with the $100 bill because you have chosen to use that money for the concert. A great question to ask is, "What is the next best use of this money?"

Since you are going to spend all of your money on paper before it is spent for real (you are, right?), it is important to always ask this question. It will help ensure that you direct your money to the items that are most important to you – your hopes and dreams.

Everyone Should Know ...
Always consider the cost of maintaining a purchase.

I remember purchasing my first car. It was an amazing 1981 Datsun B-210. It was light tan, and by the time my brother and I were through with it, it had amazing features such as rust, a broken dashboard and a hole in the passenger side floor.

My twin brother and I bought the car from our father. He made a deal with us that if we drove it for a year and did not receive a ticket or get into an accident that was our fault, he would give us back the purchase price.

Since my brother and I were perfect angels, we managed to avoid being ticketed or causing an accident. Our father gave us the money back, but we had to use it to pay for auto insurance. I had NO CLUE how much auto insurance cost. I really had no clue how much it cost for two teenage boys. The additional cost was nearly $1,400 a year! This equals nearly $120 per month in insurance premiums. I was unprepared for this extra cost related to owning a car. I had focused only on the purchase price. I had not even considered the insurance cost. Then the property tax bill showed up for the car. Shortly after that, the car broke down. Then the battery failed.

Hopefully you see my point. Many times, there are extra costs associated with maintaining a purchase that can be very expensive. Always consider the cost of maintaining the purchase before making the purchase.

Everyone Should Know ...
Wait at least one day before making a major purchase decision.

Have you ever bought something only to regret it the very next day? If so, that feeling is called "buyer's remorse." I have found that a terrific way to avoid buyer's remorse is to wait at least one day before making a major purchase decision. If you are thinking about buying a really expensive item, wait. Breathe. Sleep on the decision. It is AMAZING how much the span of one day can change your outlook on a purchase decision. I have made a large purchase without waiting (or thinking very much), and I unfortunately experienced buyer's remorse a very long time. I have rarely had buyer's remorse when I delayed a purchase for at least one day.

It can be incredibly difficult to force yourself to wait, however. When we want something, we want it now! Remember that impulsive decisions can destroy. Impulsiveness mixed with financial decisions regularly leads to financial distress and debt.

Everyone Should Know ...
Check the details.

It is important to always check the fine print before agreeing to anything. If you do not clearly understand what a contract is saying, do not sign it until you clearly understand it.

I once had a contract placed in front of me that someone asked me to sign right away. I told them that I needed to read it first. They were very impatient with me, but I did not care because my foremost goal was to check the details. I read the contract and discovered that had I signed it, I would have given up rights to information that was very important to me. I refused to sign. I am glad I read the details.

If you purchase a house, be sure to understand the interest rates and repayment terms. Clearly outline what will be sold with the house and what will not be sold with the house. Demand that broken items be repaired.

Whenever you are presented with a contract, read it before signing it!

Everyone Should Know ...
Seek wisdom from others who have been there.

When I am pondering a major decision, I always seek out other people who have made the same or very similar decision. They have wisdom that I do not have. Most people are more than willing to share their advice. In fact, most people who have already made a similar decision enjoy the opportunity to pass on their knowledge to someone else.

Are you considering attending a college? Find someone who has attended the school and ask them questions. It is even better if you find someone who has attended the school and obtained the same degree you are seeking.

If you are preparing to purchase a car, find someone who has been through the process several times. Ask them questions. Find out what has worked best for them. Even better, ask them to go with you! Of course, you want to ensure that you seek wisdom from someone who is trustworthy and of great character.

I really like it when the person I am seeking wisdom from has gray hair or no hair at all. This means that in addition to their wisdom, they have the additional wisdom and patience that only age can provide.

Always seek wisdom before making a major financial or life decision.

Everyone Should Know ...
Always ask, "How many hours will this cost?"

When you are faced with a purchase decision, it is helpful to think about how many hours of work it will take to pay for the item and ask, "Is it worth it?"

For example, if you are considering purchasing a new cell phone that costs $200 and you earn $10 an hour, you will need to work more than 20 hours for that cell phone. Is it worth 20 hours of your work?

Think about an example where a person is considering purchasing a $10,000 car. If that person earns $10 an hour, the purchase will cost more than 1,000 hours of work. Is the car worth more than half of a year's wages?

Everyone Should Know ...
$100 saved is worth more than $100 earned.

In the previous section, I wrote that the cell phone will cost **more** than 20 hours of work. I wrote that the car will cost **more** than 1,000 hours of work.

I used the word "more" because of taxes. Taxes erode purchasing power. If you earn $100, you will have to pay taxes on that money. Chances are that you will pay $25 or more in taxes. Of the $100 you earn, you will bring home approximately $75.

However, if you find a way to save $100, you really do have one hundred dollars because you have already paid taxes. If you find a way to lower your cell phone bill by $20 a month, it is the equivalent of a $30 a month raise!

Always think about the impact of taxes when considering a purchase. In the car example in the previous section, the car cost $10,000. The person earns $10 per hour. However, taxes will reduce the net earnings to approximately $7 per hour. Instead of having to work 1,000 hours to pay for the vehicle, one really has to work $1,428! That is almost an entire year of work spent on a car that will drop in value a substantial amount. Is it worth it?

Find ways to save money, and give yourself a raise!

Everyone Should Know ...
Always ask for a better deal.

Always ask for a better deal whenever purchasing an item. It is amazing what can happen when you simply ask, "Is that the best price you can give me?" It can be uncomfortable for many people to ask for a better deal. When I was broke, I was always uncomfortable asking for a better deal. I now realize that this is one of the largest reasons that I was always broke!

When I overcame the fear of asking for a better deal, I began saving a ton of money, and I stopped being broke.

I once wanted to purchase a softball glove and softball for my wife for her birthday. I did not want an entry level glove for her; I wanted the best one the store had available. The store manager assisted me with looking through the selection of high-end gloves. I found the one that would be perfect for Jenn, and then I asked the critical question.

"What type of deal can you give me?" The answer? Fifty percent off, plus they gave me some glove oil for free!

My family was traveling back home after visiting Niagara Falls, and we were tired. We decided to stop driving for the day when we were just south of Buffalo, N.Y. I went in to the hotel and asked for the price. They told me it would cost $95.96. I told them that I would be paying cash, and asked the critical question – "What type of deal can you give me?" They gave me the room for $70. The list of deals goes on and on.

Here is the basic, fundamental fact that helps me ask for a better deal.

Everything is negotiable.

Appliances, hotel, air fare, lawn service, laundry service, cars, lumber, cable television, savings account interest rates, real estate, etc. Anything that costs money can be negotiated.

I have found that my ability to obtain a better deal is greatly improved when one or more of the following situations exist:

- Competition exists (stores selling same/very similar product)
- Off-season for that product (air conditioner purchased during winter season)
- Demand is reduced (economy causes fewer people to travel which equals better deals on travel)

Ask for a better deal and spend less money than you planned and then smile, knowing you obtained more with your money just for asking for a better deal.

Everyone Should Know ...
Cash envelopes help prevent impulsive spending.

I am a spender. I love spending money. A primary reason Jenn and I were losing with our money was because of my impulsive spending behavior. A written EZ spending plan was the key to learning how to manage our money successfully. I realized, however, that we were still impulsive with some spending categories.

We were not impulsive on items like our electricity and natural gas bills. We were not impulsive on gasoline purchases. We were not impulsively spending for cable TV.

We found that we were impulsively spending money on categories directly related to food and fun. These categories included groceries, dining out, clothing, entertainment and spending money. Do you tend to spend money impulsively in any of these categories?

I found that the best way for my family to ensure that we did not overspend what we had planned for each of these categories was to use cash instead of debit or credit cards.

Here is how it works. Before we are paid, we plan our spending on paper using the spending plan. We determine how much we are going to spend in each category and ensure that the budget is EZ. Once we have forced the budget to equal exactly zero and payday arrives, we go to the bank and withdraw cash equal to the amount we have planned for our "tend-to-be-impulsive" categories. We place this money into envelopes and put away the debit card.

Whenever we need money for these "impulsive" categories, we use the cash from the envelope. When the money runs out, we are finished spending in that category for the month. FINISHED.

We are not allowed to use the debit card or go to the ATM for more money because we have already used up the money planned for our impulsive categories. If we pull out more money, it would have to come from (robbed from) another spending category. The robbery usually means that our savings account or funding for a dream is eliminated. We refuse to do that!

Cash envelopes have helped us stick to our plan and have ensured that our dreams remain funded. This is why I am a huge fan of cash envelopes. I highly recommend that you try them out for your "tend-to-be-impulsive" categories.

Everyone Should Know ...
Be organized!

Organization is critical to sound financial management. I have found that there is a good relationship between good financial management and good organization.

I am a terribly disorganized person, except when it comes to my personal finances. My desk usually has a pile of books, articles, used coffee cups and papers lying all over it. Yet, I can tell you exactly what my bank balance is (to the penny), and I can tell you where every dime has gone for the past decade.

Why am I so focused on excellent financial organization? Because I recognize how much our financial situation impacts the rest of our life. My messy desk does not really affect anyone but me. Messy finances will impact my entire family.

Make it a habit now to balance your checkbook every month. Set a calendar appointment to remind you to prepare the next month's monthly written spending plan a few days before each month begins. Every few months, take some time to think through the upcoming year or so. Is there anything coming up that will cost a substantial amount of money? Make a plan to save enough so that you can pay cash for it and avoid debt (and compound interest working against you).

Everyone Should Know ...
Always consider the impact on net worth.

Net worth is a measure of the total value of your possessions if they were all sold and reduced to money. It is calculated by adding up the total value of your possessions and subtracting the total amount of debt owed.

In the example shown, there is a total positive net worth of $44,750. Notice that the student loan debt has no tangible value, but it has a substantial amount of liability. This does not mean that a college degree is not worth the cost. It simply means that a college degree cannot be sold, so it has no measurable asset value. It can, however, help one build net worth. I know my degrees have helped me out substantially!

Assets	Value		Liabilities	Value
House	$125,000		House Mortgage	-$85,000
Motorcycle	$4,000		Motorcycle	0
Savings Account	$5,500			
Retirement Savings	$15,250			
			Student Loans	-$20,000
Total Assets	**$149,750**		**Total Liabilities**	**-$105,000**
Total Net Worth: + $44,750				

When you make financial decisions, you will have a direct impact on your net worth.

Always ask this question before purchasing something.

Will this item go up, maintain or go down in value?

A new car will go down in value as soon as it is driven off the lot. Most new cars will lose nearly 60 percent of their value in the first three years of ownership. Many people make the mistake of asking the question, "How much is the car payment?" A better question to ask is, "What impact will this have on my net worth?"

Consider an example shown for a new car purchased for $15,000 and financed 100 percent for a five-year period at 7 percent interest.

Year	Car Value	Loan	Total Payments	Loss Of Car Value	Negative Net Worth Impact [Payments + Loss Of Car Value]
0	$15,000	$15,000	-	-	-
1	$12,000	$12,403	$3,564	$3,000	$6,564
2	$9,000	$9,619	$7,128	$6,000	$13,128
3	$6,000	$6,634	$10,692	$9,000	$19,692
4	$5,000	$3,432	$14,256	$10,000	$24,256
5	$4,000	$0	$17,821	$11,000	$28,821
6	$3,000	$0	$17,821	$12,000	$29,821
7	$2,500	$0	$17,821	$12,500	$30,321

The negative net worth impact is over $30,000, more than DOUBLE the car's cost. This example does not even consider what would have happened if the money had been invested and compound interest would have worked FOR, instead of AGAINST, the car owner.

I have shared previously about the negative net worth implications of taking two extra years of college to complete a four year degree. Not only do you have to pay for two extra years of college tuition, fees and books, but you also forfeit two years of pay. That will leave a major dent on your net worth.

The key point is to always consider the impact to net worth, not just the payments. When items go down in value, it is called depreciation. When items go up in value, it is called appreciation.

Net worth grows quickly when appreciation occurs without payments. It can even work well when appreciation occurs with payments. It never works well when depreciation occurs with payments. It is a lose-lose situation.

I have made it a practice to purchase depreciating assets that are used and have already absorbed the vast depreciation cost. A 3- or 4-year-old vehicle is still a nice vehicle these days. I am driving a 13-year-old vehicle right now. I bought it when it was three years old and had already absorbed a great deal of depreciation. I paid it off in less than three years and have driven it without payments since then. It has required only one major repair; a new transmission which cost $1,953.35. It was painful, but I have not made payments for seven years. I have come out way ahead in the net worth calculation when compared to purchasing a brand new vehicle.

Everyone Should Know ...
Discipline. Discipline. Discipline.

It is my hope that you have learned a lot by reading this book. I know that this information radically transformed my financial future. I have met with a lot of people who know this information, but they are broke.

I know people who fully understand the dangers of obtaining large quantities of debt, but they have continued to swipe their credit cards and purchase new cars with 100 percent financing. As a result, they are in a horrible financial situation that is impacting them, their children, their parents, their siblings and their friendships. They knew the dangers of debt. They knew the potential impact it could have on their lives, yet they signed up for it anyway.

There are people who clearly understand that retirement is approaching and that time matters a lot when it comes to funding retirement. Even though they knew this, they are 55 years old and have yet to save any money. It seems unbelievable that one could learn the truths of compound interest and not take advantage of it, but I meet hundreds of people a year in this exact situation.

I meet people daily who know that financial emergencies are going to happen in their lives, but have saved zero money to pay for them. They know that the car is going to break down. They know that the refrigerator is going to fail. They know that the cell phone will fall into the lake. They know that emergencies will happen, but they refuse to save money for them.

There are people who want to give money away. They love giving money away, but they cannot resist the temptation to spend the money on themselves. As a result, they end up with a bunch of stuff to look at it, but are wondering why they feel unfulfilled in life.

I have written on and on about this because I want you to clearly understand that knowledge alone will not work. Of course, there must be knowledge in order to learn what is best for you. The fact that you are reading this page tells me that you are seeking knowledge, but knowledge alone will not work. There must be application. I wish that it were easy, but it is not.

You can commit to save 15 percent of your pay, and then you will drive past a new car lot. The new car will shine at you. The car you are driving will be shown for what it is: a clunker that should be replaced by the new car. If one does not have a clear, written plan, it can be very easy to swerve into the car lot and purchase the new car with a pile of new debt.

I have found that years of proper financial management can be ruined by one hour of poor and impulsive decision-making. You can commit to give 10 percent of your money away, and then you will find a new couch that is just perfect. You will justify that the couch was a much needed item, and that you will start giving again as soon as possible. I have discovered that "as soon as possible" never has a start date and usually means that it will never start.

My challenge to you is to commit to doing whatever you say. If you know that it is right and proper ... If you know that it is wise ... If you know that this is essential to fund your plans, hopes, and dreams ... Then do it!

Everyone Should Know ...
Accountability helps ensure discipline.

If you really want to help ensure that you maintain a disciplined approach with your finances, establish accountability. Find someone who has the following characteristics:

- They have won with their own money
- They will not be trying to sell you anything
- They are available for you to seek wisdom and ask questions

I am married so I have immediate accountability built in to my life. Whenever I have a bad case of, "I want that!" Jenn usually has a bad case of, "NO!" I also have accountability built in from my investment advisor. To top it all off, I have YOU as my accountability. If all I do is teach this stuff, but I fail to follow through on it, then I would be the biggest hypocrite ever!

Accountability is not always fun and glamorous. Those who hold me accountable are free to share their thoughts with me regarding my financial decisions. This means I might not enjoy the thoughts they share with me, but I know this accountability is essential to winning with my money.

Who will hold you accountable?

Everyone Should Know ...
Tips for sustainable discipline.

There are some key tools that can be put into place to ensure that a financial plan remains disciplined and focused on applying the key financial principles.

Give Regularly
- Establish automatic drafts from paycheck
- Establish automatic drafts from bank account

On-Time Bill Payment
- Plan spending every month before month begins
- Automatic drafts from paycheck
- Automatic drafts from bank account
- Utilize on line bill payment
- Pay quarterly or annually

Avoid Debt
- Save money for emergencies – every pay period
- Save for known, upcoming expenses – every pay period
- Save for dreams – every pay period
- Use cash envelopes for impulsive spending categories
- Limit use of credit card or avoid it altogether
- Instill a rule – No money, no purchase
- Apply for every college scholarship possible
- Work a job while attending college

Invest Every Month
- Establish automatic drafts from paycheck
- Establish automatic drafts from bank account
- Meet with an investment advisor once each year

Chapter THIRTEEN

Use Financial Tools

There are many free financial tools available on the internet, and our team has made a huge effort to provide a lot of them on the IwasBrokeNowImNot.com Web site.

As you enter the real world, many of these tools can become extremely useful for you. In this chapter, I will discuss the tools that we have made available on our Web site and show you how to use each of them.

Budgeting Tools
Monthly Budget
- For those with regular income.
- The best tool to use if you are paid monthly or if you have enough money in the bank to pay ALL of the bills at the start of the month.

Weekly, Bi-Weekly, Bi-Monthly Budget
- For those with regular income.
- The best tool to use to plan every single paycheck received during the month.

Mini-Budget

- For those with sporadic income.
- Also a great tool to use for planning how "found money" will be spent. "Found money" includes tax refunds, bonuses, inheritance or money obtained from selling something.
- This is also a great tool to use for planning how much money will be spent for special events like Christmas, a wedding, a vacation or a home project.

Debt Reduction Tools

Debt Freedom Date Calculator

- This calculation is designed to provide an estimate of your Debt Freedom Date.
- Enter your debt balances and monthly payments to calculate when YOU will become DEBT-FREE!

Actual Cost Of Debt Calculator

- A more detailed version of the Debt Freedom Date Calculator.
- Enter your debt names, balances, monthly payments and interest rates. This calculator will tell you how much of your payment is actually reducing the amount you owe and how much is going to the bank!

Early Pay-Off Calculator

- Use this tool to find out how much sooner you can be debt-free by making extra payments every month.

Calculators

Known, Upcoming Expenses Calculator

- This is a great tool to determine how much you should save every pay period to ensure known, upcoming expenses and future plans, hopes and dreams are funded!

Payment Calculator

- Use this handy tool to determine what the monthly payment would be for a loan.

Retirement Nest-Egg Required Calculator

- This handy tool allows you to understand how much money you will need to retire well.
- WARNING: It will be a scary number, but if you capture the power of compound interest early, you have a great chance of achieving your goal.

Investment Value Calculator

- Use this tool to determine what your investment will be worth based on its current value and your current monthly investments.

Savings Account Balance Tracking Tool

- This tool allows you to have a summarized understanding of all your money – regardless of the number of accounts you have.
- You are able to assign all your money to specific items you are saving for and then track your monthly progress toward achieving each goal.

Pay-Off Spectaculars

- Hopefully, this book has equipped you to never have to deal with paying debt off, but in the off-chance that debt was incurred this is a fun way to track your Debt Pay-Off by breaking each debt into bite-sized pieces.

Saving Spectaculars

- A fun way to track your progress toward saving for your plans, hopes and dreams by breaking each goal into bite-sized pieces.

A FINAL WORD

Thank you so much for reading *What Everyone Should Know About Money Before They Enter The Real* World. It is my hope that it has been helpful to you and that you feel equipped to apply this information. If you make it your practice to use and apply this learning, you will be able to avoid a lot of the mistakes I made during my first 10 years in the "real world."

I have found the following steps to work well in my life, maybe it will help you.

1. Plan all my spending
2. Save money every time
3. Give money every time
4. Avoid debt
5. Use the power of compound interest
6. Carry appropriate insurance

Thanks for taking the time to read this book. If I have helped you avoid one financial mistake or make one great financial decision, I consider this effort a success. Now go forth, prosper and *accomplish far more than you ever thought possible with your personal finances.*

You CAN do this!